Earning Money

by Stuart Schwartz and Craig Conley

Content Consultant:
Robert J. Miller, Ph.D.
Associate Professor
Mankato State University

CAPSTONE BOOKS

an imprint of Capstone Press
Mankato, Minnesota

Capstone Books are published by Capstone Press
151 Good Counsel Drive, P.O. Box 669, Mankato, Minnesota 56002
http://www.capstone-press.com

Library of Congress Cataloging-in-Publication Data
Schwartz, Stuart, 1945-
    Earning money/by Stuart Schwartz and Craig Conley.
    p. cm. -- (Looking at work)
    Includes bibliographical references and index.
    Summary: Explains the advantages of earning money, how to assess one's financial
needs, and how to meet them.
    ISBN 1-56065-711-1
    1. Wages--Juvenile literature. 2. Finance, Personal--Juvenile literature.
[1. Finance, Personal.] I. Conley, Craig, 1965- . II. Title.
III. Series: Schwartz, Stuart, 1945- Looking at work.
HD4906.S38 1998
332.024--dc21
                                    97-52335
                                        CIP
                                        AC

Photo credits:
All photos by Dede Smith Photography

Table of Contents

Earning Money

People work for many reasons. One of the biggest reasons is to earn money.

Money earned at jobs is wages. Wages vary from one job to the next. For example, most factory workers earn less money than doctors earn.

Workers need to understand how earning money works. Different jobs pay workers in different ways. Workers need to know when they receive payment. They need to know how much money they will receive in each check.

Employers take out some money from workers' pay. An employer is a person or company that hires and pays workers. Workers need to understand where the money removed from their paycheck goes. Workers also need to understand how they can earn higher wages.

People work at jobs to earn money.

Chapter 2

How People Earn Money

People work at all kinds of jobs. Some people make and build objects. Some people fix objects. Other people sell objects. Many people provide services. Teachers, doctors, and waiters provide services.

Workers earn money because their work has value to other people. A worker's time is worth money. Employers pay employees for their work. Employees are people who work for employers.

Many workers have special skills or training. They may attend schools or go through training programs to learn their skills. For example, truck drivers go to school. They learn how to drive trucks. They receive licenses. The licenses show they can do their jobs. They earn money because they know how to drive trucks.

Some people make and build objects.

Chapter 3

How Wages Meet Needs

People use the wages they earn to pay for items they need. People must pay for their homes. They must pay for food, clothing, and medical care. They must pay for transportation. Transportation is the way people travel from one place to another.

Workers must decide how to use their wages. They must pay certain bills each month. These are necessary payments. Rent or house payments are necessary payments. Heat and electricity bills are necessary payments. Grocery bills are also necessary payments.

Money left over after necessary payments is disposable income. People use disposable income to buy items they want. They use it to pay for hobbies and entertainment. Some people save part of their disposable income. Some employers have programs to help employees save their money.

People use wages to pay for things they need.

Chapter 4

Budgets

Workers need to know how to live on their wages. One way workers can do this is with budgets. A budget is a plan for using money. Anyone who earns money should have a budget. A budget can also show people how much they would like to earn.

Making a budget is easy. The first step is adding all necessary payments for one month. That is the amount of money a person needs for necessary payments.

The second step in making a budget is finding the disposable income. People should look at how much they earn. They should then subtract their necessary payments from that amount. This is the amount of disposable income for each month.

Many people do not have as much disposable income as they would like. But there are ways people can decrease their necessary payments. They can live in less expensive homes. They can use less electricity.

Anyone who earns money should have a budget.

Chapter 5

Earning Higher Wages

Many people start working at jobs that pay low wages. There are ways to earn higher wages. Education helps people earn more money. Workers with high school degrees earn more than people without them. A degree is a title given by a school for completing a course of study.

Special training can also help workers earn higher wages. People can receive special training at colleges or vocational schools. Vocational schools teach practical skills for trades such as carpentry and printing. People can also learn new skills on the job.

Some workers receive raises. A raise is an increase in pay. Employers give raises to workers who do good work. They usually give raises after certain amounts of time. Many employers give raises once a year.

Training can help workers earn higher wages.

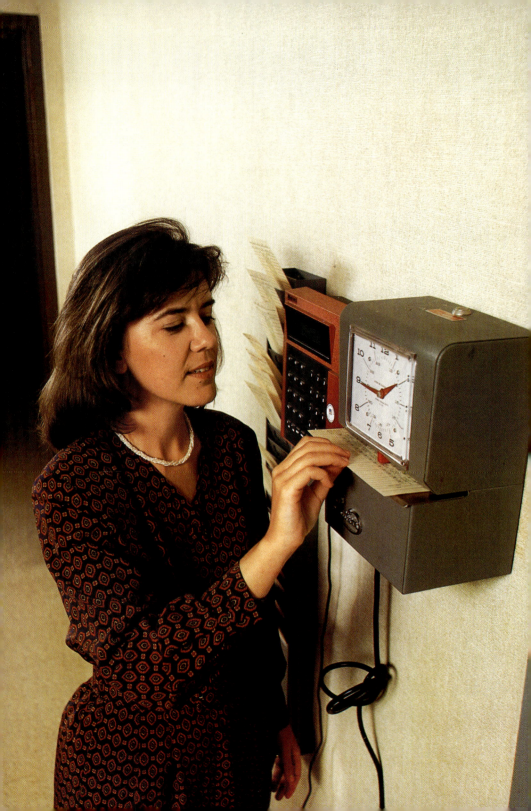

Chapter 6

Hourly Wages and Salaries

Employers pay workers in two ways. They may pay some people hourly wages. They may pay other people salaries.

People who earn hourly wages receive certain amounts for each hour they work. Sometimes these workers work more hours than usual. Extra hours are overtime. Employers pay higher hourly wages for overtime.

For example, workers at a warehouse earn $10.00 per hour. On Monday, they must fill a large order. They must work two extra hours that day. Their employer pays them extra for those two hours. The employer pays them $15.00 per hour for those two hours. The workers earn an extra $30.00 that day.

Workers who earn salaries receive set amounts of money for their work. Workers with salaries know how much money they will receive. They do not earn extra money for working overtime.

Employers pay some people hourly wages.

CURRENT PAY

Check No.	0000917
Gross Pay	460.48
Deductions	58.44
NET PAY	402.04

7.08

ILLE   FL   32614

8.37
6.63
2.78

YEAR-TO-DATE

Gross	2324.25
Federal Taxes	76.45
FICA	177.80
State Taxes	.00
Other	.00

CURRENT PAY

Check No.	0000925
Gross Pay	457.66
Deductions	57.78
NET PAY	399.88

0.31

Chapter 7

Paychecks

Most employers pay their employees with paychecks. Paychecks contain financial information. It is important for workers to understand the information on their paychecks.

Each paycheck is for a certain pay period. A pay period may be one week, two weeks, or one month. All the money earned in one pay period is gross pay. Employers subtract certain amounts of money from gross pay. These amounts are deductions. The money workers receive after deductions is their net pay.

For example, a secretary makes $800 every two weeks. Her gross pay is $800. Her employer subtracts $200 for certain payments. Her net pay is $600.

Paychecks show gross pay and net pay. They show how many hours employees worked. They show if employees used vacation or sick time during the pay period.

Paychecks show gross pay and net pay.

...URITY R	DEPT.	CHECK NUMBER	DA PA
-5122	5070	20650	10/1...

DESCRIPTION	YTD DEDUC...
CREDIT UNION	2100
A D & D PRE TAX FLEX	7...
DENTAL PRE-TAX FLEX	29
MEDICAL PRE-TAX FLEX	
VISION/HEARING PRE-T	
CHILDMEDICAL	280
SRIP 401K BASIC (MAT	1492

Deductions

Employers take certain deductions out of every paycheck. The biggest deductions are for taxes. Employers deduct money for federal, state, and local taxes.

Another deduction is for the Federal Insurance Contributions Act (FICA). This is a social security tax. The money taken out for FICA goes into a government fund. The federal government uses money from this fund to help people who have retired. The government also uses money from this fund to help people who are disabled.

Employers may take out other deductions, too. Some employers pay for part of workers' medical insurance. Workers pay for the rest. Employers deduct money from each paycheck to pay for the insurance. Some workers can ask their employers to take out more money. Employers can put it into a savings account.

Employers take deductions out of paychecks.

Chapter 9

Benefits

Some workers earn benefits. A benefit is a payment or service in addition to a salary or wages. Paid vacation and medical insurance are examples of benefits.

Different employers offer different kinds of benefits. Some employers pay for part of employees' medical and dental insurance costs. Some employers pay for all of these costs. Employers may help employees pay for child care. Almost all employers give employees paid vacation and paid sick days.

Education is another benefit. Some employers offer classes at work. Employees can learn new skills at these classes. Some employers pay for employees to take classes at schools.

For example, store owners may pay for sales clerks to take classes about using new computers. Trucking companies may pay for truck drivers to learn about new safety rules. Employees benefit from these classes.

Some employers pay for employees' medical insurance.

Chapter 10

Long-Term Benefits

Employees often receive long-term benefits from their employers. Long-term benefits help employees over a long period of time.

One long-term benefit is a retirement plan. Many employers offer retirement plans. They set aside money for each employee in a fund. Employees receive their money throughout their retirement.

For example, an employer sets aside $50 of an employee's pay each month. The employer puts it in a fund. The employee also pays $50 to the fund each month. After one year, the employee has $1,200 in the fund. After 10 years, the employee has $12,000 in the fund.

Life insurance is another long-term benefit. Some employers pay for employees to have life insurance. Life insurance is money paid to a chosen person if a worker dies. The employee chooses who will receive the money. Life insurance helps families when a family member dies.

Employees receive money from their retirement funds throughout their retirement.

Other Benefits

Wages and benefits are positive parts of working. Most people also work because they enjoy it. Work gives people new challenges. It helps them learn new facts and ideas.

Most people feel good when they do a job well. Doing good work gives workers self-esteem. Self-esteem is a good feeling about oneself. Teachers feel good about helping students learn. Sales clerks feel good about helping people choose items they want. Hair stylists feel good about helping people look their best.

Work helps people make new friends. Workers meet new people at work. People who work together get to know each other. They often share similar goals. They may also share similar interests outside of work.

Workers meet new people at work.

Chapter 12

Earning Money Helps You

Earning money can help you feel good about yourself. Earning money helps you know you can meet your needs. It helps you know you can buy items you want. Earning money also helps you see that your skills are valuable.

Workers must understand how earning money works. You must know how much you earn and when you get paid. You must understand your paychecks and all the information they contain. You must make sure you understand the benefits you earn. You can make sure your paychecks are correct if you understand these things.

Workers can learn how to earn higher wages. Education helps many workers earn higher wages. You can look into taking classes at schools. You can talk to your employers about learning new skills at your job.

Earning money can help you feel good about yourself.

Words to Know

benefits (BEN-uh-fitss)—payments or services in addition to a salary or wages

deductions (di-DUHK-shuhnz)—money taken out of a worker's pay

disposable income (diss-POH-zuh-buhl IN-kuhm)—money left after necessary payments

gross pay (GROHSS PAY)—all the money a worker earns in a pay period

hourly wages (OUR-lee WAY-juhz)—money paid for each hour of work

life insurance (LIFE in-SHU-ruhnss)—money paid to a chosen person if a worker dies

necessary payments (NESS-uh-ser-ee PAY-muhnts)—bills that people must pay each month

net pay (NET PAY)—money workers receive after deductions

salary (SAL-uh-ree)—wages paid for a certain period of time

To Learn More

Hurwitz, Jane. *High Performance Through Effective Budgeting*. New York: Rosen Publishing Group, 1996.

Longo, Tracy. *10 Minute Guide to Household Budgeting*. New York: MacMillan General Reference, 1997.

Otfinoski, Steven. *The Kid's Guide to Money: Earning It, Saving It, Spending It, Growing It, Sharing It*. New York: Scholastic, 1996.

Useful Addresses

Canada WorkInfo Net Partnership, Inc.
240 Catherine Street, Suite 110
Ottawa, ON K2P 2G8
Canada

Employment and Training Administration
200 Constitution Avenue NW
Room N-4700
Washington, DC 20210

U.S. Department of Labor
Office of Public Affairs
200 Constitution Avenue NW
Room S-1032
Washington, DC 20210

Internet Sites

America's Job Bank
http://www.ajb.dni.us

Household Budget Management
http://www.dacomp.com/budget1.html

Social Security Online
http://www.ssa.gov/

Index